Quilling Shapes

Look at all the shapes you can make with simple strips of paper!

Small Waves. Loose scrolls made with 3" strips.

Large Waves. Loose scrolls made with 6" strips.

Small Fish Head. Teardrop made with 6" strip. **Small Fish Tail.** Bunny ear made with 4" strip

Large Fish Head. Teardrop made with 9" strip. **Large Fish Tail.** Bunny ear made with 6" strip.

Seaweed. Twist quilling paper and glue.

Tiny Heart. Open heart made with 3" strip.

Small Heart. Open heart made with 4" strip.

Large Heart. Open heart made with 5" strip.

Flower. 5/8" flower punch. Loose scroll stem made with 3" strip. Grape roll (see page 4) center made with 1" strip.

Cancun - MATERIALS: *Bazzill Basics* cardstock (Aqua, Tan) • *Hot Off the Press* water print paper • 1/8" quilling paper (Green, Pale Green, Aqua, Magenta, Orange, Melon) • *Creating Keepsakes* lettering • Scallop scissors

See folding instructions for shirt on page 8.   *by Jane Cleveland*

Baby - MATERIALS: *Bazzill Basics* cardstock (Pink, Hot Pink, White) • Printed paper (*Paper Adventures, Daisy D's*) • 1/8" quilling paper (Pink, Deep Rose, Yellow, Seafoam Green) • 3/8" Seafoam Green quilling paper • Pink and Hot Pink heart die-cuts • Plastic safety pins • 3/8" letter stickers • 18" of 1/8" Pink satin ribbon

Basic Steps to Quilling

Quilling Paper comes in ⅛", ¼" and ⅜" widths.

1. Punch flowers from card-stock and handcut leaves from quilling paper.

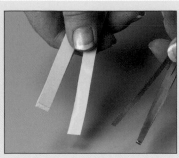

2. Choose width of quilling paper you wish to use.

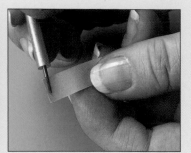

3. Insert quilling paper in quilling tool.

Basic Quilling Shapes

Tight Circle. Tightly roll the paper strip on a quilling tool. After rolling the paper, glue the loose end and remove the strip from the tool.

Loose Circle. Gently roll the paper strip on the quilling tool. Remove the strip from the tool and set it aside to loosen to the desired size. Glue loose end.

Teardrop. Roll a loose circle and glue end. Pinch one side of circle into a teardrop.

Marquise. Roll a loose circle and glue end. See the circle as a clock and pinch opposite sides at 3 o'clock and 9 o'clock to shape the marquise.

Shaped Marquise. Make a marquise and shape ends by pushing one end down and the other end up.

Bunny Ear. Roll a loose circle and glue end. See the circle as a clock, pinch at 10 o'clock and 2 o'clock and make a curved indentation at the top.

Crescent. Roll a loose circle and glue end. See the circle as a clock, pinch at 8 o'clock and 4 o'clock and shape the middle to form a crescent.

Half Circle. Roll a loose circle and glue end. See the circle as a clock, pinch at 7 o'clock and 5 o'clock and pull tight to flatten one side of the circle.

Square. Roll a loose circle and glue end. Pinch into a marquise, then turn and pinch the opposite sides. Rectangles are similar with the second pinch made closer to first pinch.

Triangle. Roll a loose circle and glue end. Pinch circle in 3 places and use your finger to form the triangle.

Scrolls

Loose Scroll. Roll one end and leave the other end straight.

Open Heart. Fold the paper strip in half and roll each end toward the center.

V Scroll. Fold the paper strip in half and roll each end toward the outside.

C Scroll. Roll both ends of the paper strip toward the center. This is similar to the open heart except the paper strip is not folded in half.

S Scroll. Roll one end of the quilling paper to the center. Turn the paper over and roll the other end to the center.

Flag. Fold the paper strip in half. Roll both ends at the same time.

Other Quilling Techniques

Grape Roll. Make a tight circle and glue the end. Gently push the center up to create a dome effect. Apply a thin layer of glue inside so the roll will retain its shape.

Spiral. Position the paper strip on the tapered needle tool near the handle and at an angle. Roll the strip tightly, spiraling down the tool. This will allow the spiral to slide off the tool's point.

Pompom. To begin, fringe quilling paper with a pair of scissors or a fringing tool. The most common widths of quilling paper to fringe are ¼" and ⅜". Roll the fringed paper into a tight circle, glue the loose end and remove from the tool.

Fringed Flower. To begin, fringe ¼" or ⅜" paper with a pair of scissors or fringing tool. Glue ⅛" paper to the end of the fringed piece. Roll ⅛" paper until it reaches the fringed piece and continue rolling until you have a tight circle. Glue the loose end and remove from tool. Use your fingers to open the flower.

4. Twist tool to roll quilling paper.

5. Remove paper and pinch sides to shape.

6. Glue quilled shapes on paper.

Husking

Husking is made by wrapping quilling paper around pins arranged in a straight line on paper. Graph paper or measured markings are used to achieve uniform distance, but differing widths can be used to make unusual patterns.

Make as many loops as the pattern or your imagination require. A drop of glue at the end of each overlap will secure the paper.

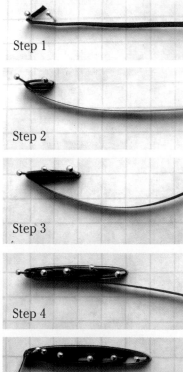

Step 1

Step 2

Step 3

Step 4

Step 5

Step 6

Large Shapes for 'Quick Quilling'

Loose Scrolls - Use to make waves, sun rays and beards.

Teardrops - Use to make wings, flowers and balloons.

Huskings - Use to make trim, fire and tree branches.

Marquise Rolls - Use for flowers, wheels and accents.

Tight Roll - Use to make flowers, insect bodies, flower centers, buttons and gumballs.

V Scroll Rolls - Use for hearts and antennae.

by Christy Lemond, Quilling by Katrina Hogan

50 Years - MATERIALS: *K&Company* paper (Tan, Green, flower print, frame) • *Close to My Heart* Pink paper • 4" strips of ⅛" Green quilling paper • *Worldwin* Pearl vellum • *Mrs. Grossman's* ⅜" letter and wedding stickers • Pop dots • 1" birch leaf punch • Green and Metallic Gold pens
TIP: Make Pink spiral roses following instructions on this page.

by Katrina Hogan

The Hogans - MATERIALS: *Bazzill Basics* cardstock (Light Green stripe, Green textured, Pink) • *Colorbök* Burgundy leather paper • ⅛" White quilling paper • *Sizzix* Green ivy die-cuts • Punches (1" birch leaf, ½" balloon) • 4 Gold brads • ⅝" Gold letter stickers
TIP: Make layered flowers following instructions on this page.

Swirl Flowers

1. With water pen make a really wet circle on the cardstock and tear out. Wet a spiral.

2. Tear out the spiral.

3. Starting from the outside end, roll until you reach the center to make spiral. Glue to secure.

Romance is in the Air.

Layered Flowers

1. Punch balloons. Roll one balloon into funnel shape with slotted tool .

2. Curl 4 balloons from side to side, cut halfway up center. Glue first piece inside open flap of funnel. Glue remaining pieces inside flap of previous piece.

3. Curl top edges of 6 to 8 balloons, cut halfway up center and glue in place.

4. Curl petals on both sides of 10 to 12 balloons, cut halfway up center and glue in place.

5. Let dry, turn over and cut off excess paper so flower will lie flat.

Make flowers with punched shapes or torn paper to add a whole new dimension to your album pages.

by Katrina Hogan

Santa
MATERIALS: *Bazzill Basics* cardstock (White, Black, Flesh) • *Paper Patch* Burgundy paper • *Windows of Time* Santa paper piecing pattern • ⅛" White quilling paper • White gel pen • Black pen

Tree - MATERIALS: *Bazzill Basics* cardstock (Brown, ¼" x 2½" strips of Green)

Ladybug
MATERIALS: ⅛" and ¼" quilling paper (†rue Red, Black)

by Christy Lemond

Beach Buddies - MATERIALS: *Close to my Heart* cardstock (Blue, Light Blue) • *Colorbök* cloud print paper • ¼" parchment quilling paper (Yellow, Pink, Dark Blue) • ⅜" quilling paper (Orange, Magenta)

Special Times and Special People

by Laura Gregory

Daddy's Angel - MATERIALS: *EK Success* star print paper • *Scrap Ease* parfait paper • Quilling paper (⅛" Bright White, ⅜" White) • *Wish in the Wind* frame • Gold thread • *Creating Keepsakes* lettering

Shirt & Pants Card
MATERIALS: *Bazzill* cardstock (8" x 12" piece of Navy Blue stripe, Red) • Print paper (*Design Originals* stars and stripes on White, denim) • Quilling paper (1/8" White and Cadet Blue, 3/8" Holiday Green) • 18" of 1/4" Gold sheer ribbon • 4 Red 3mm and 4 Clear 4mm rhinestones • Punches (5/8" flower, 1/8" circle) • Deckle scissors

Skirt & Stripe Blouse Card
MATERIALS: *Bazzill Basics* cardstock (6" x 8" piece of Dark Red, Navy Blue) • Paper (star stripe, Turquoise) • Quilling paper (1/8" White, 3/8" Holiday Green) • 5/8" flower punch • 3 Blue 3mm rhinestones • Deckle scissors

Skirt & Heart Blouse Card
MATERIALS: *Bazzill* cardstock (6" x 8" piece of White, Red) • Print paper (heart, denim) • Quilling paper (1/8" Light Blue and Soft Yellow, 3/8" Holiday Green) • 5/8" flower punch • 3 Red 3mm rhinestones • Deckle scissors

Blouse or Shirt - with No Front Seam

Size: 2:1 ratio

1. Cut a 3" x 6" rectangle of paper. With colored side up, pinch center of each short end.

2. Fold long sides to center, crease and unfold.

3. With white up, fold down top edge equal to side fold width. **4.** Fold the cut edge up to folded edge, crease and unfold.

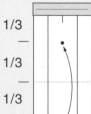

1/3
1/3
1/3

5. Fold bottom edge up 1/3 the height of figure. Be accurate.

6. Unfold so top edge is cut edge again. Turn project over.

7. Fold long sides in to meet at center along existing creases.

8. Lift loose corners at bottom center and make slanted folds.

9. Fold top edge to back on top crease.

10. Fold top corners down to meet at intersection of horizontal crease and center line.

11. Lift bottom edge and slide it under points of collar. Crease at new bottom edge.

12. The completed blouse/shirt with opening at bottom where pant or skirt may be inserted. For shirt, fold bottom sides back at an angle.

Shirt with Front Seam

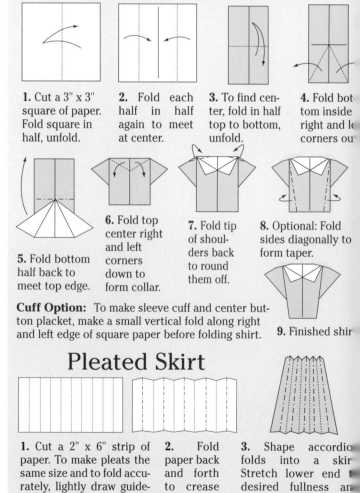

1. Cut a 3" x 3" square of paper. Fold square in half, unfold.

2. Fold each half in half again to meet at center.

3. To find center, fold in half top to bottom, unfold.

4. Fold bottom inside right and left corners ou[t]

5. Fold bottom half back to meet top edge.

6. Fold top center right and left corners down to form collar.

7. Fold tip of shoulders back to round them off.

8. Optional: Fold sides diagonally to form taper.

Cuff Option: To make sleeve cuff and center button placket, make a small vertical fold along right and left edge of square paper before folding shirt.

9. Finished shir[t]

Pleated Skirt

1. Cut a 2" x 6" strip of paper. To make pleats the same size and to fold accurately, lightly draw guidelines on the back of paper with a pencil and ruler.

2. Fold paper back and forth to crease along each line.

3. Shape accordion folds into a skir[t]. Stretch lower end t[o] desired fullness an[d] upper end to matc[h] width of bottom of shir[t].

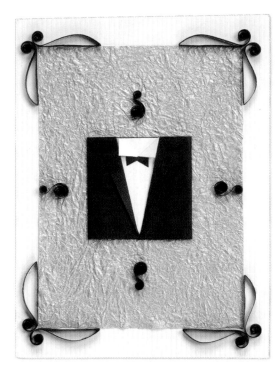

Tuxedo - MATERIALS: *Bazzill Basics* cardstock (5" x 6" piece of White stripe , Black, White stripe for shirt) • Silver crinkle paper • ⅛" Black quilling paper

Pants

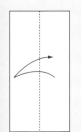

1. Cut a 3" x 6" rectangle of paper. With white side up, fold in half lengthwise. Crease and unfold.

2. Fold each half in half lengthwise to meet at center.

3. Fold in half again along existing crease.

4. Fold diagonally in half to make pants.

5. Slide pants into opening at bottom of shirt.

Tuxedo

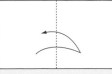 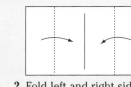

1. Cut 4" x 10" pieces of black cardstock and white cardstock. Fold in half vertically, unfold.

2. Fold left and right sides in half to meet center fold line.

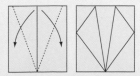 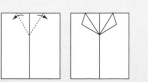

3. For coat, fold top right center corner diagonally out to right side. Repeat on left side. Tuck white shirt inside tuxedo coat.

4. For tux shirt, fold top right center corner diagonally out to the right to meet the edge of the tux lapel. Repeat on left side.

Matching Skirt & Blouse - MATERIALS: *Bazzill Basics* cardstock (6" x 7" piece of Dark Red, White) • Quilling paper (⅛" Soft Yellow and Green, ⅜" Ivory and Seafoam Green) • 3mm rhinestones (3 Red, 3 Clear, 3 Blue) • Deckle scissors

Quilling and Clothing

Combine paper folding and quilling to make a page or card filled with color and texture.

by Jane Cleveland

Western Shirt & Pants

MATERIALS: *Bazzill Basics* cardstock (8" x 12" piece of Seafoam Green, Black, White) • Paper (Silver, Black check) • ⅛" Black quilling paper • 18" of ¼" White sheer ribbon • 3 Black 3mm rhinestones • ⅛" circle punch • Deckle scissors
TIP: Make string tie with a narrow piece of quilling paper.

Fanciful Borders

Borders are easy, fun and fabulous when you combine quilled designs with punched and cut out shapes.

by Laura Gregor

Joy - MATERIALS: White *Bazzill Basics* cardstock • Metallic Gold paper • ⅛" Holiday Green quilling paper • Red paper twist • 1¾" *Dayco* Red letter die-cuts • 4 Metallic Gold photo corners

by Jane Cleveland

Flower Border - MATERIALS: *Bazzill Basics* cardstock (Lavender, White, Pink) • Quilling paper (⅛" Pale Green and Soft Yellow, ⅜" Pale Green, Yellow and Violet) • 3mm rhinestones (4 Pink, 4 Clear) • ⅝" flower punch

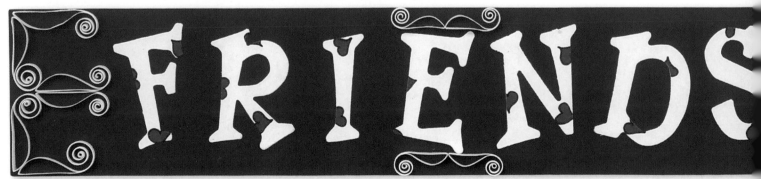

by Jane Cleveland

Friends - MATERIALS: Red *Bazzill Basics* cardstock • ⅛" White quilling paper • *Daisy D's* heart paper • 1¾" letter die-cuts

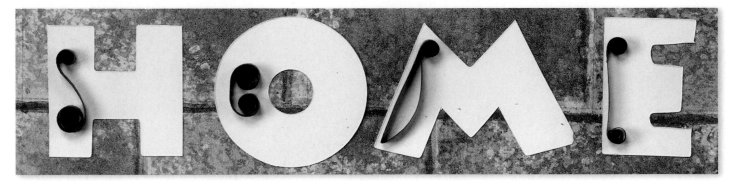

by Laura Gregory

Home
MATERIALS: *Wubie* Brick print paper • 1/8" Brown quilling paper • *Dayco* Cream 1 1/2" die-cut letters

Flower
MATERIALS: *Bazzill Basics* cardstock (Tan, Green) • 3/8" quilling paper (White, Bright Yellow, Holiday Green) • *Stampin' Up* ivy stamp • Green ink pad

White Flower Border
MATERIALS: *Bazzill Basics* cardstock (White, Light Blue) • Quilling paper (1/8" White, 3/8" White) • 6 Clear 2 mm rhinestones • 5/8" flower punch

Love Border
MATERIALS: Heart print paper • Quilling paper (1/8" White, 1/8" Red) • *Dayco* Red heart and 1 3/4" letter die-cuts • White chalk

by Katrina Hogan   by Jane Cleveland   by Laura Gregory

Gingham Tags
by Katrina Hogan

Pink Flower Tag
MATERIALS: Blue plaid paper • ⅛" quilling paper (Pink, Yellow, Green) • Beige paper twist • Yellow flower eyelet • Eyelet setter • Punches (⅛" circle, ³⁄₁₆" square)

White Flower Tag
MATERIALS: Blue plaid paper • ⅛" quilling paper (White, Gold, Green) • Golden paper twist • Yellow flower eyelet • Eyelet setter • Punches (⅛" circle, ³⁄₁₆" square)

Large Pink Flower Tag
MATERIALS: Blue plaid paper • ⅛" quilling paper (Pink, Bright Yellow, Green) • Golden paper twist • Yellow flower eyelet • Eyelet setter • Punches (⅛" circle, ³⁄₁₆" square)

by Laura Gregory

Photo Tag - MATERIALS: ⅛" Black quilling paper • Gold die-cut tag • Photo

Turtle Tag
MATERIALS: ⅛" Black quilling paper • Gold die-cut tag

Gift Tags and More

by Jane Cleveland

Snowflake - MATERIALS: Light Blue card-stock • ⅛" Light Blue quilling paper • White die-cut snowflake • ⅝" flower punch • 3mm Clear rhinestone

by Jane Cleveland

Glove
MATERIALS: ⅛" Blue quilling paper • Beige glove die-cut • Beige chalk

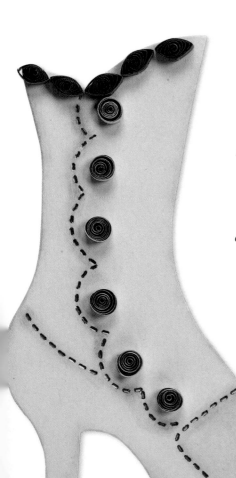

Die-cut shapes provide the backgrounds for small, quick and easy projects.

by Katrina Hogan

Baby Bottle Tag
MATERIALS: ⅛" Lavender quilling paper • Yellow baby bottle die-cut • 12" of ¼" Pink sheer ribbon • 3mm Clear rhinestone • Yellow chalk

by Jane Cleveland

Shoe - MATERIALS: ⅛" quilling paper (Lavender, Violet) • Light Blue shoe die-cut • Purple chalk • Purple pen

by Jane Cleveland

Swan - MATERIALS: ⅛" quilling paper (White, Black) • White swan die-cut

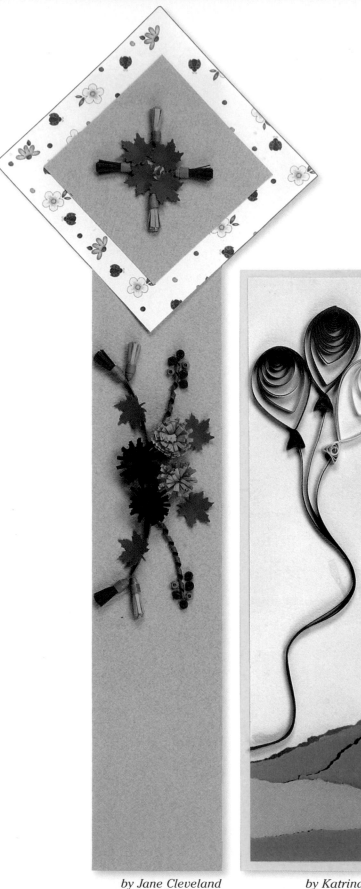

by Jane Cleveland

Tan Border
MATERIALS: *Bazzill* cardstock (Tan, Rust) • *Over the Moon Press* print paper • Quilling paper (⅛" Green, Brown, Burgundy and Deep Rose, ⅜" Burgundy and Gold) • ½" maple leaf punch

by Katrina Hogan

Balloon Border
MATERIALS: Bright Yellow *Bazzill* cardstock • *EK Success* landscape paper • ⅛" quilling paper (Violet, True Red, Yellow, Black)

by Jane Cleveland

Green Border
MATERIALS: *Bazzill* cardstock (Rust, Light Green) • Quilling paper (⅛" Periwinkle Blue, Yellow, Magenta, Cadet Blue, Holiday Green and Rust, ⅜" Holiday Green) • Miniature rake and seed packet • Gardening stickers • Decorative scissors

by Jane Cleveland

Burgundy Border
MATERIALS: *Bazzill* Burgundy cardstock • *Anna Griffin* print paper • Quilling paper (⅛" White and Soft Yellow, ⅜" Flesh and Seafoam Green) • Decorative scissors

Tip - See flower & leaf on page 3

Fanciful Borders

Delicate little border designs are a snap with quilled flowers, punched shapes and a few embellishments.

Baby Buggy Border

MATERIALS: *Bazzill* cardstock (Pink, White, Light Blue) • *Worldwin* Silver pin stripe paper • 1/8" quilling paper (White, Silver Grey, Pink, Light Blue) • 8" of 1/8" Light Blue satin ribbon • Pop dots • Decorative scissors

TIPS: To weave buggy body, tape strips of Pink quilling paper side by side. Weave with alternating Blue and White strips. Glue on White cardstock and cut out buggy shape.

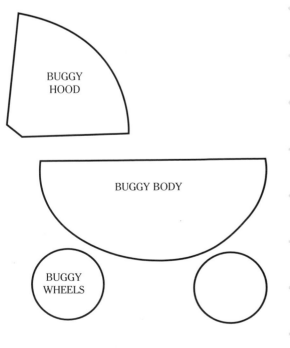

BUGGY HOOD

BUGGY BODY

BUGGY WHEELS

by Jane Cleveland

Pink Border

MATERIALS: *Bazzill* cardstock (Pink, Blue, Yellow) • Quilling paper (1/8" Meadow Green and Yellow, 3/8" Meadow Green, Pale Pink and Cadet Blue) • 4 Pink 3mm rhinestones • 5/8" flower punch • Decorative scissors

by Laura Gregory, quilling by Jane Cleveland

Tag, You're It!

by Laura Gregory

Party Tag & Envelope - MATERIALS: 'Happy Birthday' print paper • Green tag die-cut • ⅛" quilling paper (Yellow, Black) • ¼" Red curling ribbon • Computer generated message

by Jane Cleveland

Yellow Flower Tag - MATERIALS: Yellow die-cut tag • Quilling paper (⅛" Rust, Ivory and Green, ⅜" Rust and Green)

by Jane Cleveland

Blue Tag - MATERIALS: Blue tag die-cut • ⅛" White quilling paper

Thank You Tag - MATERIALS: Turquoise cardstock • Pink tag die-cut • Quilling paper (⅛" Yellow and Turquoise, ⅜" Soft Green) • ½" Black letter stickers • 2 Clear 3mm rhinestones

by Jane Cleveland

Special Occasion Tags

Decorated tags are perfect for invitations, greeting cards and thank you notes.

by Laura Gregory

Photo Tag - MATERIALS: Dark Blue die-cut tag • ⅛" Ivory quilling paper • Photo

by Laura Gregory

Birthday Tag - MATERIALS: Yellow tag die-cut • ⅛" quilling paper (Turquoise, Black) • Red 'Happy Birthday' sticker

by Jane Cleveland

Gold Tag - MATERIALS: Gold tag die-cut • Quilling paper (⅛" Pale Green and Soft Yellow, ⅜" Turquoise and Pale Green) • 3 Yellow 3mm rhinestones • Computer generated message

by Laura Gregory, quilling by Jane Cleveland

Party Page - MATERIALS: *Bazzill* cardstock (Green, Gold, Red) • ⅛" quilling paper (Lavender, Violet) • *Gussies* party print paper • *Accu-Cut* die cuts (Gold mask, 1¼" Gold letter, 1½" Red) • Rhinestones (One 12mm Clear, 4 Clear 9mm, 2 Clear 8mm x 18mm teardrops, 32 assorted 6mm)

TIPS: Make mask decorations following Husking instructions on page 5. See mask pattern on page 22.

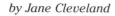

by Jane Cleveland

by Jane Cleveland

Green Butterfly
MATERIALS: Green butterfly die-cut • ⅛" quilling paper (Black, Yellow, Turquoise) • 1" long Black paper bead

Aqua Butterfly
MATERIALS: ⅛" quilling paper (Black, Orange, Aqua) • ½" long Black paper bead

by Katrina Hogan

Red Flower
MATERIALS: ¼" parchment quilling paper (Red, Green) • 10mm Clear rhinestone

Ladybug - MATERIALS: Red ladybug die-cut • ⅛" Black quilling paper

by Laura Gregory

Cheerleader - MATERIALS: *Paperkins* doll and clothes die-cuts • ⅛" White quilling paper • 2 Black 6mm pompoms • ½" Black letter sticker

by Katrina Hogan

by Jane Cleveland

Stocking - MATERIALS: Red and White stocking die-cuts • ⅛" quilling paper (White, Holiday Green, Yellow, True Red) • Black pen

by Laura Gregory

Mitten - MATERIALS: Cardstock (Yellow, Violet) • Blue mitten die-cut • ⅛" quilling paper (True Red, Yellow, Violet) • Black pen

Die-Cuts

Accent die-cuts or create dimensional shapes with quilling for spectacular results!

by Jane Cleveland

Corn

MATERIALS: Green corn die-cut • ⅛" Gold quilling paper • Natural paper twist

by Laura Gregory

Christmas Tree

MATERIALS: Green tree die-cut • ⅛" quilling paper (Gold, True Red, White) • Dark Green fiber • Red bow

by Jane Cleveland

Gumball Machine - MATERIALS: Green gumball machine die-cut • ⅛" quilling paper (White, Yellow, True Red, Black, Meadow Green, Violet, Cadet Blue)

Borders and More Borders

You can make a border for every season or event with quilled designs and a few simple accents.

by Katrina Hogan and Laura Gregory

Winter Border - MATERIALS: *Bazzill Basics* cardstock (Blue, White) • ⅛" quilling paper (White, Black) • *Sizzix* 1¼" Blue and White letter die-cuts • *ZBarten* Party ice and Iridescent glitter • 6 Silver 1" split rings

by Ruth Ann Warwick

Thanksgiving Border - MATERIALS: *Bazzill Basics* cardstock (Dark Green, Ivory) • ⅛" quilling paper (Gold, Yellow, Orange, True Red) • Paperkins doll and clothes die-cuts • Six assorted Beige buttons • Foam tape • Green and Brown pens

by Ruth Ann Warwick, quilling by Jane Cleveland

Duck Border - MATERIALS: Bazzill Basics cardstock (Blue, Brown, Dark Brown) • ⅛" quilling paper (Orange, Yellow) • Green grass die cut • Foam tape • Brown and Green chalk

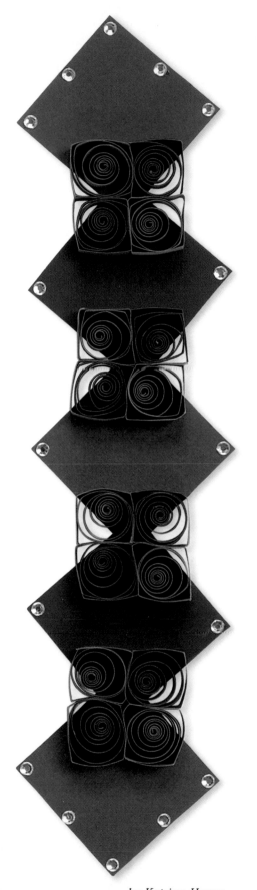

by Katrina Hogan

Border
MATERIALS: *Bazzill Basics* cardstock (Blue, Dark Green) • 12" strips of 3/8" quilling paper (Periwinkle Blue, Holiday Green) • 6 Clear 4mm rhinestones

by Laura Gregory

Heart Border
MATERIALS: *Daisy D's* Pink paper (solid, dot, stripe) • *Adornaments* Hot Pink fiber
TIP: Cut a 1/4" x 12" strip of Pink for quilling paper.

by Laura Gregory

Snowman Border
MATERIALS: Blue cardstock • 1/8" quilling paper (Black, White) • *Creative Imaginations* Heart and snowflake stickers

Quilling for Scrapbooks & Cards **21**

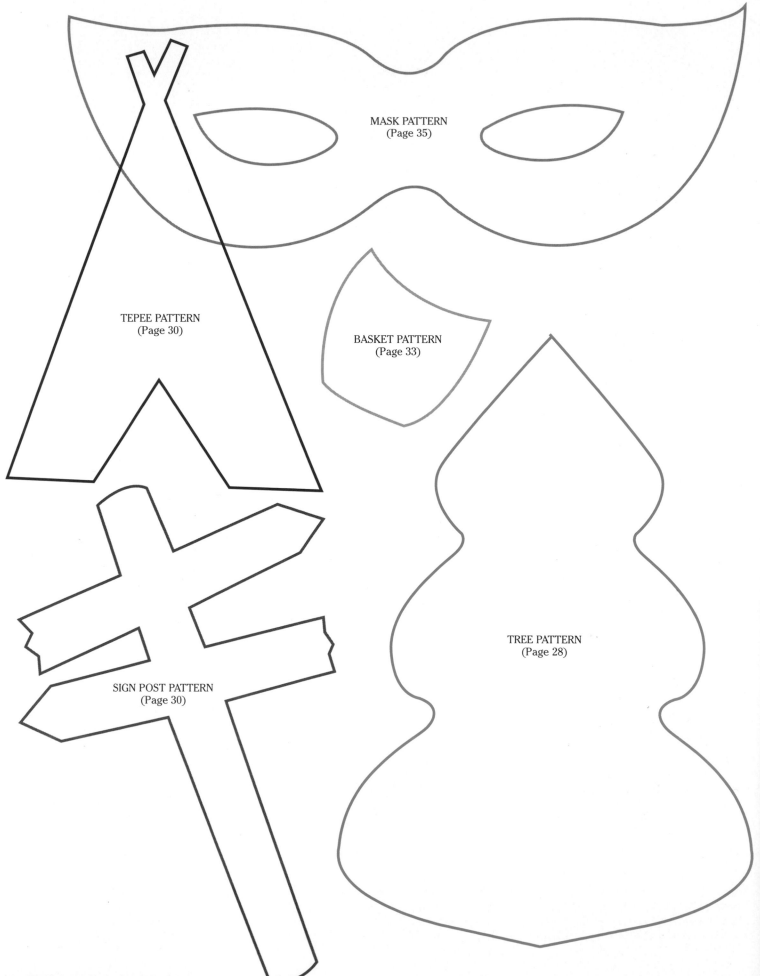

MASK PATTERN
(Page 35)

TEPEE PATTERN
(Page 30)

BASKET PATTERN
(Page 33)

TREE PATTERN
(Page 28)

SIGN POST PATTERN
(Page 30)

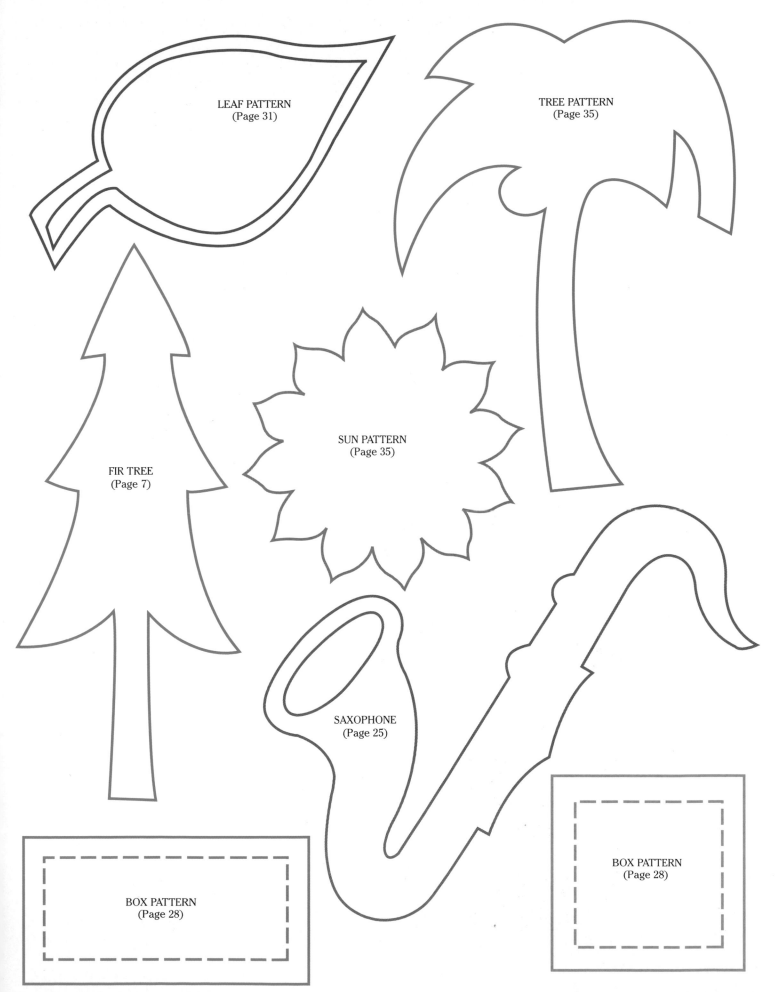

LEAF PATTERN
(Page 31)

TREE PATTERN
(Page 35)

FIR TREE
(Page 7)

SUN PATTERN
(Page 35)

SAXOPHONE
(Page 25)

BOX PATTERN
(Page 28)

BOX PATTERN
(Page 28)

Special Occasions

Add a few quilled shapes and your pages come alive with visual interest.

by Laura Gregor
quilling by Jane Cleveland

See folding instructions on page 8.

Banquet Page
MATERIALS: *Bazzill Basics* cardstock (White, Black, Ivory) • *Pixie Press* paper (Black/Gold print, Gold, Silver print vellum) • 1/8" White quilling paper • 2 Clear 6mm rhinestones • 3/4" Black letter stickers • Computer generated journaling • Decorative scissors

by Laura Gregory

Too Cute Page
MATERIALS: *Bazzill Basics* cardstock (Black, Grey cloud print) • 1/8" Black quilling paper • *Stamping Station* Black and Purple house die-cuts • 3/4" Black die-cut letters • *Magic Mesh* (large square holes and small square holes) • Grey chalk • Black pen
TIPS: Spider is made with 6" strip for body, 2" strip for head and 1" strips for legs.

by Jane Cleveland

Music Page

MATERIALS: *Bazzill Basics* cardstock (Black, White) • ⅛" quilling paper (Black, White) • *It Takes Two* and *Gussies* music print paper • *Accu-Cut* Black saxophone die-cut • Computer generated lettering

TIPS: Music notes are marquise shapes made with 3" strips. Saxophone keys are loose circles made with 2" and 4" strips.

Saxophone pattern on page 22.

by Laura Gregory
quilling by Katrina Hogan

Wedding Page

MATERIALS: *Bazzill Basics* cardstock (Sage Green, Burgundy) • *Robin's Nest* butterfly print vellum • ⅛" quilling paper (Green, Pink, Burgundy) • 4 Gold rose nailheads • 4 Gold photo corners

TIPS: Make quilling pieces as follows:

Bell - Two 24" strips glued end to end, rolled and shaped.

Clapper - 12" strip rolled in tight scroll.

Bow Center - 24" strip rolled tight.

Pink Flower - Nine 9" strips rolled into teardrops.
    Center - 8" strip grape roll.

Burgundy Flower - Eight 12" strip rolled into teardrops.
    Center 8" strip rolled tight.

Pink Buds - 3" strip rolled into teardrops.

Leaves - 6" strips rolled into marquise shapes.

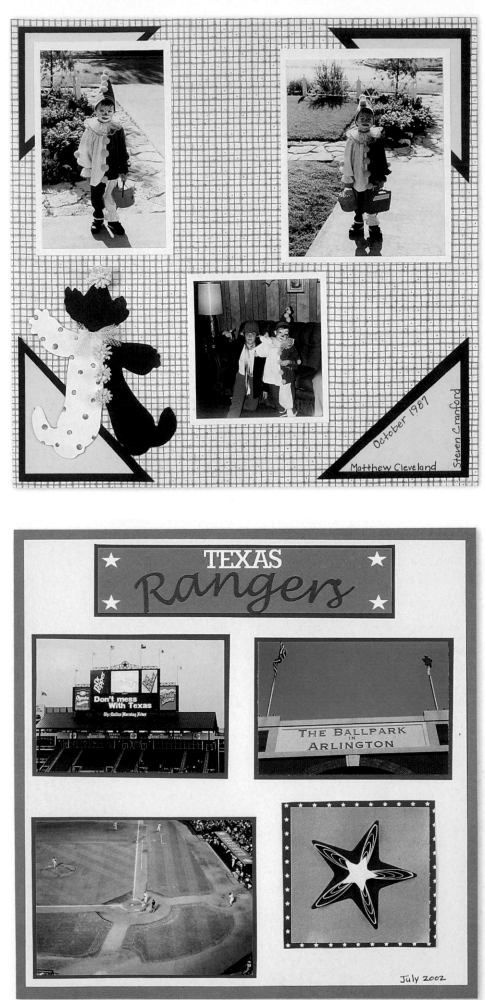

by Laura Gregory, quilling by Jane Cleveland

Clown Page

MATERIALS: *Bazzill Basics* cardstock (Yellow, Navy Blue, White) • *Daisy D's* Blue plaid paper • ⅜" Yellow quilling paper • *Accu-Cut* Navy Blue and *Daisy D's* White dot paper clown die-cuts • ½" x 3" strip of White tulle • Needle and thread • Black pen

TIPS: Gather tulle with needle and thread and glue on neck of die cut clown.

CLOWN PATTERN
©ACCU-CUT™

by Laura Gregory

Rangers Page

MATERIALS: *Bazzill Basics* cardstock (Red, White, Blue) • *Paper Patch* Red star print paper • *Worldwin* Silver paper • ⅛" White quilling paper • *Stamping Station* die-cuts (star, letters, small star) • 1" White foam star • Black pen

TIP: Make quilled star following Husking instructions on page 5.

by Laura Gregory & Katrina Hogan

Flag Page
MATERIALS: *Bazzill Basics* cardstock (Red, White, Blue) • *Sonburn* Red stripe print paper • ⅛" quilling paper (Red, White, Blue) • *Anna Griffin* ribbon • 6 Gold star nailheads • Computer generated journaling

TIPS: Make flag pieces as follows:
32 Red 6" strips rolled into loose circles.
22 White 6" strips rolled into loose circles.
16 Blue 6" strips rolled into loose circles
9 White 4" strips rolled tight.

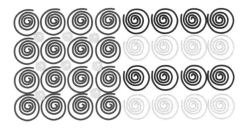

HELPFUL HINT
Make a large flag with 8" strips.
Make smaller flags with 4" or 6" strips.

July 4, 2002
Autumn and Allie Gregory
Photo by Tricia Kay Photography

Autumn Gregory
November 2001

More Special Occasions

A clown, a star, a flag and a frame… these pages are excellent examples of quilling for scrapbooks!

by Laura Gregory
quilling by Jane Cleveland

Horse Page
MATERIALS: *Robin's Nest* print paper (Blue plaid, Denim) • Cardstock (Red, White, Blue) • *Wish in the Wind* Red & Blue frame • ⅛" White quilling paper • *O'Scrap* cowboy hat die-cut • 2 Silver star nailheads • Computer generated journaling

Holidays & More

Wrap a tree, add a border, attach a tag or scatter quilled designs... the results are cheerful and bright!

by Katrina Hogan

Devin Page -
MATERIALS: *Bazzill Basics* cardstock (Blue, Green, Red, Gold) • *K&Company* Tan background paper • 1/8" quilling paper (Holiday Green, True Red, Black, Gold) • *Sizzix* 1¼" Blue letter die-cuts • Chalk (Gold, Red, Green, Blue)
TIP: Use 12" of quilling paper to make squares.

by Laura Gregory

HoHoHo Page
MATERIALS: *Bazzill Basics* cardstock (Green, Yellow, Red, White) • *Sonburn* Red stripe paper • Quilling paper (1/8" Burgundy, Seafoam Green, Bright Yellow, True Red, Cadet Blue, Pale Pink, Silver, White and Gold, 3/8" Burgundy and White) • *Accu-Cut* Green 'HoHoHo' die-cut • Green felt • One Red and 3 White 6mm pompoms • *Adornaments* Red fiber • 10 small Gold jump rings • 6mm Clear rhinestone • Computer generated journaling • Green chalk
TIPS: Make quilling ornaments as follows:
Tops - 2" strips rolled tight.
Ornaments - 4" strips rolled into teardrops.
    2" strip rolled into square.
    2" strip rolled into marquise.
    2" strips rolled into fringed flowers.
Star - 4" strips roll into marquise shapes.
Glue tops on flowers, square and marquise. Glue jump rings on paper ornaments and pompoms.
    Box and tree patterns on pages 22 & 23.

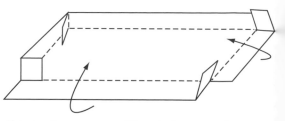

Using patterns on page 22, make boxes as shown above. Cut and glue corners in place.

PASSA DA PASTA ?

ITALY TRIP 2001

by Jane Cleveland

Passa Da Pasta? Page
MATERIALS: *Bazzill Basics* cardstock (Green, Red, Dark Green, White) • *Pixie Press* Italy print paper • ⅛" quilling paper (True Red, Brown, Purple) • ½" maple leaf punch • 8" pieces of ⅛" satin ribbon (Red, White, Green) • Computer generated lettering
TIPS: Make quilling pieces as follows:
Grapes - 4" strips grape rolls.
Branch - Spiral roll.
Frames - 4" strips rolled into flags.

by Jane Cleveland

St. Patrick's Day Page
MATERIALS: *Bazzill Basics* cardstock (Green, Ivory, Orange, White) • *Paper Adventures* heart print paper • Quilling paper (⅛" Green, ⅜" Green) • Green and heart print heart die-cuts • ½" flower punch • 3mm rhinestones (8 Green, 5 Clear) • Green pen • Computer generated lettering
TIPS: Make quilling pieces as follows:
Clover - 6" strips rolled into open hearts.
Stem - 1" strip.

St. Patrick's Day

WHAT'S NOO AT THE ZOO ?

A visit to
Fort Worth
Zoo
1985

Add natural elements in a snap with quilled branches, vines, trees and a glowing campfire.

by Jane Cleveland

What's Noo at the Zoo? Page

MATERIALS: *Bazzill Basics* cardstock (Green, Black, Ivory marble, Ivory) • *NRN Designs* animal print paper • 1/8" quilling paper (Brown, Green, Tan) • 5/8" paw print punch • Computer generated lettering

TIPS: Make quilling pieces as follows:
Leaves - 4" strips rolled into marquise shapes.
Branches - 4" strips rolled into spirals.
Nuts - 2" strips rolled into tight circles.

Outdoor Fun & School Days

by Jane Cleveland

Camping Page

MATERIALS: *Bazzill Basics* cardstock (Green, Red, Gold, Tan) • *Robin's Nest* tree print paper • 1/8" quilling paper (Green, Brown, Yellow, Orange) • *Accu-Cut* die-cuts (Red tepee, Tan sign) • 5/8" paw print punch • Brown chalk • Pens (Green, Black , Brown)

TIPS: Make tree and fire following Husking instructions on page 5. Tree trunk and fire logs are spirals of different lengths.

Sign post and teepee patterns on page 22.

Class Page

MATERIALS: *Bazzill Basics* Green and Brown cardstock • *Over the Moon Press* print cardstock (large apple, small apple) • ⅛" quilling paper (Brown, Holiday Green) • *Paperkins* doll and clothes die-cuts • Apple die-cut • 12" of ⅛" White satin ribbon • Chalk (Brown, Red, Blue) • White gel pen

TIPS: Make quilling pieces as follows:
Doll Hair - 4" strips rolled into marquise shapes and 4" strips rolled into spirals.
Apple Leaf - 4" strip rolled into marquise.
    Stem - 2" strip rolled into spiral.

by Jane Cleveland

Autumn Page

MATERIALS: *Bazzill Basics* cardstock (Rust, Tan, Ivory) • *K&Company* leaf print paper • Quilling paper (⅛" Orange, Brown, Tan and Green, ⅜" Lavender, Violet, Soft Yellow and Tan) • *Stamping Station* Orange pumpkin die-cut • ½" maple leaf punch • Computer generated journaling • Orange chalk • Scallop scissors

TIPS: Make quilling pieces as follows:
Pumpkin - 4" strips rolled into marquise shapes.
    Stem - 4" strip rolled into teardrop.
    Eyes - 2" strips rolled into triangle.
    Nose - 4" strip rolled into triangle.
    Mouth - 1" strip folded.
Pompom Flower - 12" strip rolled into pompom.
Fringed Flower - 2" of ⅛" Rust and 6" of ⅜" paper rolled into fringed flower.
Star Flower - 4" strips rolled into marquise shapes.
Center - 2" strips rolled into grapes.
    Leaf patterns on page 23.

by Laura Gregory • quilling by Jane Cleveland

Special Times and People

Commemorate holidays with darling quilled hearts and bunnies.

by Laura Gregory,
quilling by Jane Cleveland

Easter Page

MATERIALS: *Bazzill Basics* cardstock (Light Blue, Yellow) • *Colorbök* Green paper • *Wish in the Wind* Pink & White frame • *Paper Adventures* dot print paper • Quilling paper (⅛" White, Pink, Yellow, Pale Green, ⅜" Light Blue, Pale Green) • *Accu-Cut* Lime Green tag die-cut • 1¼" Lime Green die-cut letters • 4 Pink 3mm rhinestones

TIPS: Make quilling pieces as follows:
Bunny Body - 15" strip rolled into loose circle.
    Head - 9" strip rolled into loose circle.
    Feet - 4" strips rolled into teardrops.
    Hands - 3" strips rolled into teardrops.
    Inner Ears - 4" strips rolled into teardrops.
    Outer Ears - Follow Husking instructions on page 5.
Bow - 12" strip rolled into spiral and pulled loose.
    Center - 4" strip rolled into loose circle.
Flower Stems - 3" strips rolled into spirals.

by Jane Cleveland

Oh Baby Page

MATERIALS: *Bazzill Basics* cardstock (Blue, Grey, White) • *Paper Adventures* paper (Blue marble, Blue plaid, heart plaid, Blue check) • Quilling paper (⅛" Light Blue, Sky Blue, Seafoam Green and Yellow, ⅜" Seafoam Green) • Blue and Blue marble heart die-cuts • ½" White letter stickers • 18" of ⅛" White satin ribbon • 4 plastic safety pins

TIPS: Make quilling pieces as follows:
Hearts - 3", 4", 5" strips rolled into open hearts.
Flower Centers - 1" strips rolled into grapes.
    Stems - 3" strips rolled into spirals.
    See folding instructions for shirt on page 8.

by Laura Gregory

Valentine's Day Page

MATERIALS: *Daisy D's* Pink paper (strip, dot, solid) • ⅛" Pink quilling paper • 8 Clear 9mm rhinestones • Computer generated journaling • Decorative scissors • Foam tape

TIPS: Roll 6" strips into open hearts.

by Jane Cleveland

Eggs Page

MATERIALS: *Bazzill Basics* cardstock (Lavender, Yellow, Pink, Light Blue) • *Paper Adventures* Blue dot paper • ⅛" quilling paper (Yellow, Light Blue, Pink, Light Pink, White, Black, Tan, Lavender, Ivory) • Egg die-cuts (Pink, Yellow, Light Blue, Light Green) • 3mm rhinestones (4 Clear, 2 Purple) • Paper crimper • Decorative scissors • Black pen

TIPS: Make basket by taping Tan strips side by side on a work surface. Weave with Ivory strips and glue ends to secure. Glue woven strips to White cardstock and cut out basket shape. Make edge and handle with Ivory quilling paper.

Make quilled shapes as follows:

Rabbit Body - 15" strip rolled into loose circle.
    Head - 9" strip rolled into loose circle.
    Feet & Ears - 4" strips rolled into teardrops.
    Hands - 3" strips rolled into teardrops.
    Nose - ½" strip rolled into loose circle.
Flowers - 2" strips rolled into marquise shapes.
    See basket pattern on page 22.

by Ruth Ann Warwick
quilling by Jane Cleveland

Cute Page

MATERIALS: *Bazzill Basics* cardstock (Green, Bright Yellow) • *Daisy D's* Yellow plaid paper • Quilling paper (⅛" Black, True Red, Gold, Meadow Green) • ¾" Black letter stickers • ⅛" circle punch • Foam tape • Black pen

TIPS: Make quilling shapes as follows:
Caterpillar Head - 12" strip rolled tight.
 Body - 10" strips rolled tight.
 Antennae - 3" strip rolled into V scroll.
 Feet - 1" strips folded into feet and legs.
Bee Wings - 6" strips rolled into teardrops.
 Body - 6" strip rolled into teardrop
 Head - 4" strip rolled tight.
 Antennae - 2" strip rolled into V scroll.
Ladybug Wings - 12" strips rolled into half circles. Add punched dots.
 Head - 4" strip rolled into loose circle.
 Antennae - 2" strip rolled into V scroll.

by Laura Gregory

Happy Birthday Page

MATERIALS: *Bazzill Basics* cardstock (Yellow, Green, Red, White) • *Sonburn* stripe paper • Quilling paper (⅛" True Red, Gold, Meadow Green) • Letter die-cuts (1¼" Red, 1½" stripe) • Black embroidery floss • Black pen

TIPS: Make balloons with 12" strips rolled into open teardrops and 4" strips rolled into bunny ears.